LEONARD J. ARRINGTON
MORMON HISTORY LECTURE SERIES
No. 23

# OPERA AND ITS VOICES
# IN UTAH

*by Walter B. Rudolph*

*Sponsored by*

Special Collections & Archives
Merrill-Cazier Library
Utah State University
Logan, Utah

Published by Merrill-Cazier Library
Distributed by Utah State University Press
Logan, UT 84322

# ARRINGTON LECTURES

# FOREWORD

## F. Ross Peterson

The establishment of a lecture series honoring a library's special collections and a donor to that collection is unique. Utah State University's Merrill-Cazier Library houses the personal and historical collection of Leonard J. Arrington, a renowned scholar of the American West. As part of Arrington's gift to the university, he requested that the university's historical collection become the focus for an annual lecture on an aspect of Mormon history. Utah State agreed to the request and in 1995 inaugurated the annual Leonard J. Arrington Mormon History Lecture.

Utah State University's Special Collections and Archives is ideally suited as the host for the lecture series. The state's land grant university began collecting records very early and in the 1960s became a major depository for Utah and Mormon records. Leonard and his wife Grace joined the USU faculty and family in 1946, and the Arringtons and their colleagues worked to collect original diaries, journals, letters, and photographs.

Although trained as an economist at the University of North Carolina, Arrington became a Mormon historian of international repute. Working with numerous colleagues, the Twin Falls, Idaho, native produced the classic *Great Basin Kingdom: An Economic History of the Latter-day Saints* in 1958. Utilizing available collections at USU, Arrington embarked on a prolific publishing and editing career. He and his close ally, Dr. S. George Ellsworth, helped organize the Western History Association, and they created the *Western Historical Quarterly* as the scholarly voice of the WHA.

While serving with Ellsworth as editor of the new journal, Arrington also helped both the Mormon History Association and the independent journal *Dialogue.*

One of Arrington's great talents was to encourage and inspire other scholars or writers. While he worked on biographies or institutional histories, he employed many young scholars as researchers. He fostered many careers as well as arranged for the publication of numerous books and articles.

In 1972, Arrington accepted appointments as the official historian of the Church of Jesus Christ of Latter-day Saints and the Lemuel Redd Chair of Western History at Brigham Young University. More and more Arrington focused on Mormon, rather than economic, historical topics. His own career flourished with the publication of *The Mormon Experience,* co-authored with Davis Bitton, and *American Moses: A Biography of Brigham Young.* He and his staff produced many research papers and position papers for the LDS Church as well. Nevertheless, tension developed over the historical process, and Arrington chose to move full-time to BYU with his entire staff. The Joseph Fielding Smith Institute of History was established, and Leonard continued to mentor new scholars as well as publish biographies. He also produced a very significant two-volume study, *The History of Idaho.*

After Grace Arrington passed away, Leonard married Harriet Horne of Salt Lake City. They made the decision to deposit the vast Arrington collection of research documents, letters, files, books, and journals at Utah State University. The Leonard J. Arrington Historical Archives is part of the university's Special Collections. The Arrington Lecture Committee works with Special Collections to sponsor the annual lecture.

# Preface

I would describe my stature as a musicologist beyond that of "armchair," to more like "carousing." When offered, Utah's operatic history was unknown to me. Still, I did not inhale before accepting.

The most compelling evidence exposed was the level of musical talent within Utah's immigrant society. How remarkable that virtually every element of a cross-sectioned European society was represented by those who arrived in Utah prior to the completion of the Trans-Continental Railroad —including music and serious vocal arts. This is Utah's heritage.

Credit must be expressed to all those artists whose musical commitment was of sufficient intensity that they were unstoppable by the unknown frontiers of America's West and the citizens of what is now Utah.

In the live presentation given in Logan on September 28, 2017, tenor Stanford Olsen sang three arias, collaborating with Dallas Heaton at the piano: "Ecco, ridente in cielo" from *The Barber of Seville* (Gioacchino Rossini); "En fermant les yeux" (also known as "Le rêve" [The Dream] from *Manon* (Jules Massenet); and "E lucevan le stelle" from *Tosca* (Giacomo Puccini).

Stanford Olsen, a Utah native, is Professor of Music and Chair of the Department of Voice in the School of Music at the University of Michigan. He sang 160 performances with the Metropolitan Opera. It was his name that brought the crowd to the Logan Tabernacle. His part on the program was a rich conclusion and reward for all who were there.

In April 1984, I was in New York City on radio business. I took the opportunity to attend a performance at the Metropolitan Opera during

LDS General Conference weekend, Saturday, April 7. The opera was *Francesca da Rimini* by Riccardo Zandonai, a seldom-performed work, which I had analyzed for my Master's thesis. I was invited into the Saturday matinee radio broadcast booth during intermission by the Met's Broadcast Producer, Ellen Godfrey.

While there, and as the intermission feature was beginning, an urgent telephone call came into the booth. The report was that the Met's matinee radio broadcast signal had been lost to all of its New England affiliate radio stations. The problem was quickly rectified, but not before Ellen had a moment to look at me and pass blame. The momentary replacement of the Met's opera signal to those New England stations had been LDS General Conference. Of such are Utah's tales and wonders about this all-encompassing art form called *opera*.

The following I graciously thank and recognize for their consent to be interviewed. Each, individually, has contributed to the operatic scene in Utah. These contributions are either acknowledged within this paper or otherwise provided inspiration to the project.

James Arrington
Susan Arrington Madsen
Michael Ballam
Cohleen Bischoff
Ariel Bybee
Elaine Clark
David Dalton
Karen Lynn Davidson
Crawford Gates
Roger Miller
JoAnn Ottley
Leslie Peterson
James Prigmore
LeGrand Richards, Jr.
Joanne Rowland
Dorothy Thomson
Ardean Watts

Support provided to me by Special Collections Departments in the libraries at Utah State University, the University of Utah, and Brigham Young University was always immediate, substantial, and graciously helpful. Equal appreciation goes to the LDS Church History Library and Utah State Historical Society.

Becky L. Thoms (Head of Digital Initiatives) and Trina Shelton (Administrative Assistant to Bradford Cole), both at the Merrill-Cazier Library, Utah State University, provided exemplary assistance.

Most important was the endless patience of my wife, Marilyn. She assisted in every possible manner imaginable, as she always has.

Genealogical lines are sufficiently pronounced in our state that there will be more than a few who may read this, then shake their heads in disbelief that I failed to name their ancestor or friend of significant musical prowess. To all who are negatively inclined for any omissions, I apologize.

There are more "Utah operatic *voices*" awaiting discovery. My hope is that what I have compiled will be sufficient to inspire others to continue.

Walter B. Rudolph
February 12, 2018
Orem, Utah

# WALTER B. RUDOLPH

Walter B. Rudolph is a retired broadcaster and musicologist. He was General Manager of KBYU-FM, *Classical 89* (Brigham Young University—Provo, Utah) for most of 35 years. There he initiated broadcasts of Utah Opera, Utah Festival Opera, and The Grand Teton Music Festival. He produced numerous radio programs and documentaries, believing you can no more educate an audience to classical music without entertaining them than you can whip water to cream. He relishes discussing factual foibles along with more salient musical matters, which at least partially explains his collection of music-related comic strips.

Under his direction came the first syndicated broadcasts in the United States of the NHK Symphony, Tokyo. *The Russian Messiah* (1991) was recorded in Kazan, Tartarstan by KBYU-FM. It was the first performance of Handel's *Messiah* given in Russia in the 20th century. Celebrating the fall of the Iron Curtain, it was broadcast in Europe, Asia, and North and South America.

Rudolph's namesake connection to Christmas became the 8-part radio drama *The Christmas Chronicles* (2010), which he commissioned from Utah playwright Tim Slover.

His interest and rapport with the Bayreuth Festival in Germany led to radio programs and lectures on both Richard Wagner and his descendent family. He has also been the subject of a Wagnerian interview by noted British radio producer/author Jon Tolansky. He made *Adventures with Wagner in Jazz* with jazz-great Valerie Capers. In 2013, he gave a full-day presentation for Richard Wagner's 200th birthday before a select audience at WFMT in Chicago.

His degrees are in vocal performance and musicology with an emphasis in verismo opera. An accomplished operatic voice will stop him in his tracks. His early singing idols were Giorgio Tozzi and Hans Hotter, both of whom became subjects of radio documentaries. He interviewed Dietrich Fischer-Dieskau for a 6 part series on his career and German *Lieder*. Producing five radio programs on the great Swedish tenor, Jussi Björling, resulted in his two-term stint as President of the Jussi Björling Society-USA, on whose board he continues to serve. In 2011, he was invited to speak about Björling's American career at the Jussi Björling Centenary Congress in Stockholm, Sweden.

Seen on his old license plate frame was *Born again in Bayreuth–Wotan Lives*. Today, his license plates still disclose his musical passions, which have always been encouraged and matched by his much better half, Marilyn Cloward. They are the parents of three sons and a daughter.

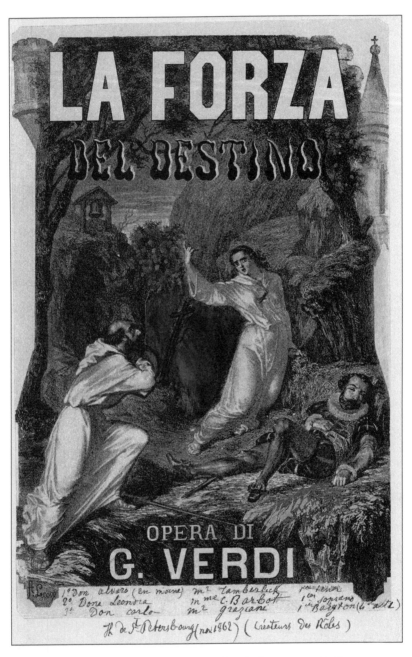

Giuseppe Verdi's *La forza del destino*, (by Alexandre Charles Lecocq, c. 1870)

# OPERA AND ITS VOICES IN UTAH

It was March 4, 1960. Leonard Warren sang his aria, "Morir tremenda cosa," (To Die is a Tremendous Thing) and fell to the floor of the stage at the Metropolitan Opera, dead from a cerebral hemorrhage. He was only 48. The opera was Giuseppe Verdi's *La forza del destino*—*The Force of Destiny*.[1] I was in junior high school in Cody, Wyoming. I knew enough about opera that I needed to know more.

In 1975 I saw *The Force of Destiny* at the Met.[2] Backstage after the performance, I knocked on the dressing room door of Bonaldo Giaotti, the basso who had sung the role of the Priest, Padre Guardiano. "Good evening," he said pulling his priestly beard from his face, "but if you've come for confession, you are too late!" Being "too late" for over forty years, I have saved it all for this paper—perhaps my own appointment with "destiny," and the confession of my "operatic sins."

In 1597 a royal marriage was celebrated in Italy with an elaborate vocalized stage production. Yes, it was for the elite and rich, and it is remembered as the first opera. Today, opera is for the masses. I like to think of it as fine dining in the performing arts—with all the courses.

Opera is the art form unifying all others. The voices (or elements) of opera are expert backstage execution, an orchestra, scenic and costume design, dramatic detail, lighting and stagecraft, dance, and the final and defining ingredient—singing—in multiple languages. Not just a pleasant voice, but one trained to sing beautifully and project over an entire orchestra. No microphones allowed.

Today's German superstar tenor, Jonas Kaufmann says:

> ... the voice ... enhances music.... It is probably ... the instrument with which and because of which music was ... invented. And it's also the most direct link between one soul and another.... When we (singers) perform a song, we pack ... genuine emotions into the voice, to achieve a specific emotional effect....[3]

It is the trained operatic voice which allows opera to exist. To experience the excess and emotion of opera enhances our perspective and helps us go home as more reasonable individuals.

The Edward W. Tullidge *History of Salt Lake City* states, "Musical development is very much the index of civilization, and its variations of quality, the signs of national character."[4] Musically, Utah's pioneer immigrants had talents akin to some of the world's finest musicians. But isolated in Utah, they were unknown in the professional music world. They made choirs, bands, orchestras, a theatre, recitals, concerts, musicals, operetta, oratorio, and opera.

Utah's instrumental music was represented by William Pitt and his Nauvoo Brass Band, and later, Domenico Ballo, who had been bandmaster at West Point. This Italian convert to the Church of Jesus Christ of Latter-day Saints was trained in the Conservatory in Milan, Italy. He soon had Utah pioneers listening to Mozart, Meyerbeer, and Rossini—all operatic composers of the first rank.[5]

David O. Calder initiated vocal music training in what was then called Deseret. Critics had accorded approval to his *Messiah* and *Creation* performances in Scotland before he came to Utah in 1851. Calder organized two music classes in 1861, each with 200 members to whom he introduced the Curwen tonic sol-fa method—a means of learning to read music. He arranged and printed the books they used. Then he organized two more classes of the same size. Using this Curwen notation, he began teaching the choruses of Vincenzo Bellini's *La sonnambula*, which would have become Utah's first performed opera had it not been for an outbreak of diphtheria. Caring for his family broke his own health and ultimately took the lives of five of his children.[6]

On March 6, 1862, the Salt Lake Theatre was dedicated. Its location was the northwest corner of State Street and First South. It seated 1,500 of Salt Lake City's 12,000 residents and was the only theatre west of the Mississippi.[7]

1862 was also the year that Giuseppe Verdi went to St. Petersburg, Russia for the premiere of his 23rd opera, *La forza del destino*, which was commissioned by the Russian Imperial Theatre.

A year later, Professor John Tullidge arrived in Utah from England. A noted tenor, Tullidge had turned down an offer to be trained in Italian opera by the world's foremost tenor, Giovanni Mario, who had told him, "I never knew the English had voices till I heard yours." Instead, Tullidge became a concert singer, conductor, and composer. His first concert in Salt Lake City was a program of oratorio arias. Nine years later he fell to his death on the stairs in the Salt Lake Theatre.[8]

Opera officially arrived in

The Howson Opera Troupe brings Opera to Utah, 1869

Utah with The Howson Opera Company in 1869—a family of singers from Australia, who performed *The Grand Duchess of Gerolstein* by Jacques Offenbach.[9]

It was Utah's George Careless who conducted *The Grand Duchess*. Careless had joined the Mormon Church at the age of 11 in England, where he was born in 1839. He was a near contemporary of Tchaikovsky and Dvorak. Trained as a violinist at London's Royal Academy of Music, Careless was a performing professional by the age of 23.

He came to Utah and in 1865 was invited to meet with Brigham Young, who called him to be:

> ... the Chief Musician of the Church; [also] to take the Tabernacle Choir and the Theatre Orchestra and lay a foundation for good music. From the day [Careless] arrived, [that force of] destiny marked him for a foremost place among those appointed to train and uplift the musical taste of Utah's Mormon settlers.[10]

The Salt Lake Theatre Orchestra had 16 players. Nine weren't up to the task. Careless wanted it reduced to seven or he would resign. And he wanted them paid. "Three dollars a night each, *in cash*." The approval came directly from Brigham Young.[11]

George Careless could improvise music on-the-spot during a performance. He once failed to remember the need to compose the music for a new production. Careless set to work, composing the 40 required pieces in two days. So prodigious were his gifts that he was offered similar work in Nevada for $1,000 a month in gold. He rejected the offer. He had not left England for Utah to be lured elsewhere.[12]

Soprano Lavinia Triplett had preceded Careless to Zion. They had performed together professionally in England, and eventually they married. Her voice was of entrancing beauty. "All who ever listened to the noble melody of her voice knew that she had received from nature one of those gifts which are conferred but a few times throughout the course of centuries."[13] Lavinia died in 1885, only 38 years old; her husband lived until 1932.

Colonel J. H. Mapleson was a British impresario whose opera company toured Britain and the United States in the 19th century. His company stopped over in Salt Lake City in early March 1884, on its way to San Francisco.[14] His star soprano was Adelina Patti, who Giuseppe Verdi described as "the finest singer who ever lived."[15]

Patti visited the Tabernacle, hoping to persuade local powers to allow a concert in that building on their return trip. She praised its attributes to President John Taylor. When told it was only a place of worship, Patti then launched into enthusiastic praise of Mormon doctrines, expressing a strong wish to join the Mormon Church. Her cajoling worked. The returning train stopped in Salt Lake City for the grand performance on April 1, 1884.[16]

Adelina Patti sang only four solos on the program, two of which she encored: "Il bacio" by the company's conductor, Luigi Arditi, and "Home, Sweet Home" from the opera, *Clari, the Maid of Milan* by Sir Henry Bishop. Duty done, she quietly returned to the train before the concert ended. Patti had achieved her goal of giving the first concert in the Tabernacle. Nothing more was said about her attraction to the doctrines of the LDS Church or her thoughts toward baptism. The train left that same night.[17]

After all the hoopla about Patti being first to sing in the Tabernacle, there are at least two sources indicating that Anna Bishop had already given the first concert in the Tabernacle on July 14, 1873, at the invitation of Brigham Young.[18] She was the estranged wife of Sir Henry Bishop, the composer.

Nearly a quarter of Utah's population was English. So it was natural that Gilbert and Sullivan's *HMS Pinafore* created a furor. It was repeated "times without number," when it was produced by George Careless in 1879. Over the next few years, *Trial by Jury, The Sorcerer, Pirates of Penzance, Iolanthe, Patience,* and *The Mikado* all played in Salt Lake City.[19] Copyright was an issue at the time. A book published in England could be legally copied and sold in America without author or publisher payment. Sir Arthur Sullivan thought otherwise: "It seems to be their opinion that a free and independent American citizen ought not to be robbed of his right of robbing somebody else."[20]

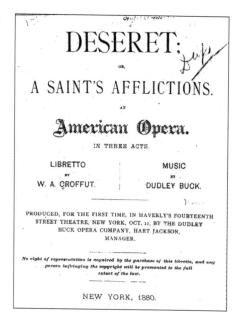

Libretto cover to Dudley Buck's *Deseret*, 1880

October 11, 1880, Haverly's Fourteenth Street Theatre in New York City premiered a new opera by the New England composer, Dudley Buck. William A. Croffut was the librettist. This polygamy parody was titled *Deseret, or A Saint's Affliction.* The cast included: Elder Scram, who is the husband of 24 wives and father of 1 child; and Joseph Jessup, the dishonest Indian Agent, who attacks polygamy—obviously the story's villain.[21]

To see the strength of the influence of Gilbert and Sullivan, consider this text for Jessup's aria:

*I fear that the Lieutenant may discover my duplicity,*
*And not believe that I was driven to it by necessity;*
*So I will git me up and git and fly from this vicinity,*
*And take with me a specimen of Mormon femininity.[22]*

Croffut and Buck had written a comedy. But *The New York Times* saw it in the darkest of terms:

.... about Mormonism there is a repulsive nastiness, which the efforts of several professional humorists have not succeeded in making amusing. The victims of this wretched system are not attractive subjects for comedy.... As to the music, Mr. Buck ... is a well-known ... competent writer, but ... his musical abilities have been wasted.[23]

The Welshman, Evan Stephens, became the 8th conductor of the Salt Lake Tabernacle Choir in 1890, but not before having a bout with the operatic bug in 1889. Founding the Stephens Grand Opera Company, he produced Sir Michael Balfe's *The Bohemian Girl,* Gaetano Donizetti's *Daughter of the Regiment,* and Friedrich von Flotow's *Martha.*[24]

*The Daughter of the Regiment* requires a tenor with exceptional high C's for its famed aria, "A mes amis." Robert C. Easton, noted for his "magnificent, heart-reaching lyric tenor voice," took the role.[25] At the dedication of the Salt Lake Temple, it was Easton who first sang the Eliza R. Snow hymn, "O My Father," to the melody Mormons use today.[26]

In 1901, W. A. Spaulding, editor of the *Los Angeles Times,* wrote specifically about Utah's baritone, Heber S. Goddard:

> (He) ... possesses a voice not only of marvelous range, but also of phenomenal power and sweetness.... He is already acknowledged the finest baritone in the West, and, if musical prophecy is fulfilled, Salt Lake will soon have reason to be proud of a native son in the constellation of operatic stars.[27]

Goddard died of pneumonia only three years later.[28]

The Australian prima donna, Dame Nellie Melba, came to Salt Lake City in 1898 to sing with Evan Stephens and the Mormon Tabernacle Choir. When Stephens told her he wished to have the choir sing his signature piece for her, "Let the Mountains Shout for Joy," she told him, "I'll listen to it because it's yours, not because it's Mormon."

After hearing it, her response was "... you've touched me to the depths of my very soul." Before she left Salt Lake City, she asked Stephens how many wives he had, not knowing he was a confirmed bachelor, to which he suavely replied, "Not so many, Madame Melba, but what I could take one more."[29]

The Opera Workshop space at Brigham Young University is named for B. Cecil Gates, the brother of soprano Emma Lucy Gates, both grandchildren of Brigham Young. Her 1902 review by *The New York Times* was not very promising:

> ... Miss Lucy Gates [is] a young American soprano, of whom nothing can be set down in praise, except that she has a serviceable voice. Her entire method, however, from her tone-placing to her vocalization needs reconstruction. One seldom hears a singer with a more complete catalogue of the vices of singing.[30]

Intensive study perfected her technique. In 1909 Gates received a five year contract with the Royal Opera in Berlin, where she sang secondary roles to Frieda Hempel. After two years in Berlin, she requested and was granted a transfer to the Royal Opera in Cassel (Kassel), where her reviews began to sparkle. She became a prima donna. During this period she sang over 50 roles from Rossini to Bizet and Mozart to Wagner.[31] Having returned to America in 1914, World War I ended her German career. New doors soon opened in America.

From 1915 to 1928, she and her brother, B. Cecil Gates, organized and toured the Lucy Gates Grand Opera Company. The repertoire included *La traviata, Faust, Roméo et Juliette, Rigoletto, Carmen,* and *Cavalleria rusticana.*[32] In 1916 she signed a five-year recording contract with the Columbia Gramophone Company, becoming a top-selling artist with a discography of 46 songs and arias.[33]

*La traviata,* with *Fräulein* (Lucy) Gates, Cassel, Germany, 1912. Photograph courtesy of L. Tom Perry Special Collections, Harold B. Lee Library, Provo, UT.

Her recording of "The Doll Song," from *The Tales of Hoffman* by Jacques Offenbach, demonstrates her technical achievements, combined with her coloratura voice and musicianship.[34]

In 1919, Henry Theophilus Finck, music critic for the *New York Evening Post,* wrote:

> Whatever the operas [chosen], they will afford opportunities to hear the loveliest soprano voice now on the operatic or concert stage, American or foreign. Two years ago I wrote on this page that Miss Gates had a more beautiful voice and more finished vocal art than the much advertised Mme. Galli-Curci. This statement aroused a surprising amount of discussion .... I now go a good deal further and say that Miss Gates is the equal of the greatest prima donnas the country has produced—such artists as Emma Eames, Lillian Nordica and Geraldine Farrar.[35]

A Richard Wagner fever possessed America at the turn to the 20th century. Wagner had forbidden any stagings of his 1882 Holy Grail opera,

SALT LAKE THEATRE
GEO. D. PYPER, Manager

Monday, Tuesday, Wednesday and
Wednesday Matinee
MESSRS. MARTIN & EMERY'S
Reverent, Artistic and Sumptuous Presentation
of ▮▮▮▮ Wagner's Sacred Festival Play

PARSIFAL

IN ENGLISH
Adapted by Wm. Lynch Roberts. The most
noted production of the century.

NEXT ATTRACTION

THE ROSCIAN COMIC OPERA CO.

Thursday, Friday and Saturday Evenings.
Matinees Washington's Birthday and Saturday.
In revivals of old time popular Comic
Operas, including

Thursday Matinee and Night  .    THE MIKADO
Friday Evening   .    .    .    .    EL CAPITAN
Saturday Matinee   .    .    THE BOHEMIAN GIRL
Saturday Evening   .    .    .    A DIAVOLO
Prices 25c to $1.00, Mat. ▮   ▮c,
Children 25c anyw▮▮

Martin & Emery's version of Richard Wagner's
*Parsifal* in Salt Lake City. "The most noted
production of the century."

*Parsifal*, outside of the Wagner theatre in Bayreuth, Germany, for which it had been specifically composed. In 1884, B. B. Young, a baritone student of George Careless, sang in a concert performance of *Parsifal* in London. Young had gone to England for further training. There he met and married the daughter of Alberto Mazzucato, who for 11 years had been music director of the famed La Scala Opera Company in Milan, Italy.[36]

The Metropolitan Opera staged *Parsifal* on Christmas Eve in 1903, breaching the German copyright not recognized in the United States. Suddenly, everyone in America succumbed to endless newspaper commentaries on *Parsifal*. Viewing *Parsifal* rose to bucket-list prominence. Salt Lake City, Logan, and Provo all responded to the publicity of the Martin and Emery touring company production, which played multiple years and multiple performances in Utah.

It was advertised as "Martin & Emery's Reverent, Artistic and Sumptuous Presentation of (Richard) Wagner's Sacred Festival Play *Parsifal* in English. The most noted production of the century." Reverent, artistic, sumptuous, and sacred; the most noted production of the century—but never is there a cast listing, review, or clarification of what Martin and Emery were really presenting. Consider these promotional commentaries on the Martin and Emery production of *Parsifal*:

- the grandest of all music compositions
- the grandest drama ever written[37]
- his peerless dramatic spectacle, *Parsifal*
- the wonderful magnetism of Wagner's genius[38]
- correct historical costuming, architecture, and appointments
- a competent coterie of artists will be seen in the principal roles
- all of the Baireuth customs will be carried out[39]

In 1908 the *Logan Republican* reported that a Mrs. Leiter traveled with the Martin and Emery production. She held wardrobe responsibility for the 1882 premiere of *Parsifal,* produced by Wagner himself. She had been sent from Bayreuth to assist with this production.[40] Wagner himself labeled *Parsifal* as a *Bühnenweihfestspiel, or* "stage-consecrating festival play." Martin and Emery never used the word "opera," but they did occasionally slip in the word "play" or "festival play." In reality, Martin and Emery were taking advantage of all the free publicity that had mushroomed around the Metropolitan Opera's 1903 production. But instead of anything musically related to Wagner's *Parsifal,* it was nothing more than a modified translation adapted for a dramatic presentation.

The November 7, 1908, *Deseret Evening News* reads: "As everyone knows, *Parsifal* is the dramatized version of the great Wagner opera, and the last time it was given in Salt Lake it left a deep impression."[41]

Other than the misleading publicity, little can be found to sustain these "most noted" rants about this production. *Goodwin's Weekly* offered differing thoughts a week later:

> Remembering the reception given *Parsifal* at the Theater the past two seasons by Salt Lakers, one would think that the powers, whoever they be, ... would wake up to the fact that this order of theatrical rot has about spent its strength in these valleys .... *Parsifal*, as dramatized in prose, is stale, uninteresting and deadly tiresome.
>
> The presenting company worked like a lot of amateurs, forgetting their lines, stamping around the stage, mouthing their words and declaiming unintelligibly. The scenery was worn out and costumes ditto. Outside of this there was not much the matter with the show.[42]

Newspaper postings of the repertoire chosen by John J. McClellan for his regular Tabernacle organ recitals demonstrate the ongoing *Wagnermania* that was still present in Salt Lake City.

| | |
|---|---|
| "Prelude" from *Parsifal* | "Evening Star" from *Tannhäuser* |
| "March" from *Meistersinger* | "Overture" from *Tannhäuser* |
| | (October 2, 1907)[43] |

A chorus from *Die Meistersinger* was on the program for the first broadcast of the Mormon Tabernacle Choir in 1929.[44] During the early years of the Hill Cumorah Pageant, the prophet Abinadi was burned at the stake to "The Ride of the Valkyries," also by Wagner.[45]

In 1882 (the year *Parsifal* premiered), the Walker Opera House opened across the street from the current Capitol Theatre—overwhelming the older Salt Lake Theatre. George Careless conducted the debut concert with local talent singing arias of Bellini and Giacomo Meyerbeer. The orchestra played the overtures to Franz von Suppé's *Pique Dame* and Gioacchino Rossini's *William Tell.*[46] (Imagine hearing the *William Tell Overture* before there was a *Lone Ranger.*) The

*Salt Lake Telegram*—September 9, 1922

Walker burned in 1891. Six years later, the Salt Lake Opera Company formed with Lucy Gates, Robert Easton, and Heber Goddard on the roster. It closed in 1911.[47]

Radio broadcasts began in Salt Lake City in May 1922. Five months later, the first non-professional radio broadcast of an opera in the United States was heard over KDYL in Salt Lake City.[48] It was Puccini's *La bohème*. Rosamonda Hart was Mimi and her son, Cedric Elliott Hart, sang the tenor role of her lover, Rodolfo. The orchestra consisted of piano, violin, xylophone, drums, and horn. A narrator explained the flow of action during the 90 minute transmission.[49]

Professional Grand Opera for Utahns came mostly from touring companies in the early 20th century, including the Boston Lyric, Savage, and San Carlo Opera companies.[50] Visiting solo artists also left their mark, as they still do today. Consider recitals by Johanna Gadski, Lillian Nordica, and Lotte Lehmann; Kirsten Flagstad and Helen Traubel, plus Ernestine Schumann-Heink, Rosa Ponselle, John McCormack, Lawrence Tibbett, John Charles Thomas, and Nelson Eddy.[51]

The dazzling Russian bass, Feodor Chaliapin, was scheduled in *The Barber of Seville* in the Salt Lake Tabernacle on January 21, 1927.[52] Trouble began with the decision that there would be no scenery—only draperies. Then the entire production, including Chaliapin, was cancelled over a rule forbidding costumed performances in the Tabernacle.[53]

Scene from the Sun dance Opera

*The Sun Dance* by William F. Hanson. BYU Production, 1915. Photograph courtesy of L. Tom Perry Special Collections, Harold B. Lee Library, Provo, UT.

Even the great Swedish tenor, Jussi Björling, sang in Provo in 1939 and then appeared with the Ogden Tabernacle Choir in 1945.[54] Björling's great-great aunt, Hanna Sund, had converted to Mormonism and preceded him to Utah in 1866.[55]

Brigham Young University had its own unique impresario in Herald R. Clark, Dean of Commerce. His legacy to BYU was an imposing array of visiting artists. He would find touring musicians headed west and then contact the artists' management, promising both a stellar audience and acoustic in the Provo Tabernacle. Then he would say something like:

> And while we cannot pay a regular fee, a stop in Provo is on the way to California. So what we offer is simply icing on the cake. And the artist can stay in my home and my wife will provide home-cooked meals and her home-made Mormon pickles.[56]

Ezio Pinza was one who tasted those pickles. During his recital, this matinee idol became the target of a bat determined to find the source of the sonorities rising from Pinza's throat.[57] Or was it the pickles?

Among the singers on Herald R. Clark's list were Paul Robeson, Tito Schipa, Eleanor Steber, Jussi Björling, Ramon Vinay, Pierre Bernac (with Francis Poulenc), George London, Leopold Simoneau, Victoria de los Angeles, Eileen Farrell, Jan Peerce, Leontyne Price, and even Anna Russell.[58] Other artist appearances included no less than Béla Bartók and Sergei Rachmaninoff.

William F. Hanson was a professor of music at BYU. His five act opera, *The Sun Dance*, had a simple romantic plot built around the traditional Sun Dance of the Sioux. It premiered in Vernal on February 20, 1913, with a success requiring 22 more performances given between Payson and Salt Lake City, each with a minimum of 10 encores. Hanson had grown up with a desire to preserve the music and traditions of the Native American Utes.[59]

Gertrude Simmons Bonnin was his librettist, a Sioux woman who became a noted author. Their collaboration brought together authentic customs and melodies expressed in Hanson's Germanic European musical style. Its success even took it to Broadway.

> On April 27, 1938, heavy curtains ... opened to reveal ... the New York Light Opera Guild's annual American opera, *The Sun Dance*. The sophisticated audience straightened, sniffed, and whispered to their neighbors as a sharp, clean scent drifted out among them. It was pungent, [burning sagebrush], invigorating, crisp as mountain air. The aroma evoked a land of simple savages and a time that seemed as far-removed from ... Broadway as Shangri-La.[60]

Hanson is best remembered today for his song for children, "I Have Two Little Hands," well-known among members of the LDS Church.[61]

From 1930–1933, J. Reuben Clark, Jr. served as ambassador from the United States to Mexico. While thus engaged, at least two significant, yet ancillary, events occurred. Best known was his call into the First Presidency of the Church of Jesus Christ of Latter-day Saints. The other was his introduction and instantaneous connection to opera.

The evening of January 25, 1931, was spent in the home of a Mexican diplomat, listening to a recording of Giuseppe Verdi's *Aïda*. Ambassador Clark was 60 years old. The experience was of such immediacy as to prompt a letter to his daughter in Washington, D. C. It instructed her to go to a record store and spend an afternoon listening to *Aïda*; then hearing and comparing *Bohème, Rigoletto,* and *Tosca,* to see if they favorably compared to *Aïda*. She was then to purchase them all, if passing muster.

As a member of the First Presidency of the LDS Church, Clark revealed little interest in music. He told local bishops he disliked the music of Bach.

In contrast, he would invite LDS Apostles Harold B. Lee, Henry D. Moyle, and Marion G. Romney to his home for dinner and then listen to full-length recordings of Donizetti's *Lucia di Lammermoor* and Verdi's *Nabucco.*[62]

The postlude at President Clark's funeral in the Tabernacle was "Siegfried's Funeral March" from *Die Götterdämmerung* by Richard Wagner, played by Alexander Schreiner on the organ.[63]

In January of 1961, Leonard Kastle's opera, also titled *Deseret,* was televised nationally by NBC Opera Theatre. The libretto was by Anne Howard Bailey. *The New York Times* called the story of a Mormon girl, who is the prospective 25th wife of Brigham Young, "the most expert and convincing opera yet produced by American authors."[64]

The cast included Judith Raskin and John Alexander as the young lovers, and Kenneth Smith as a spiritually dignified Brigham Young. There was no judgment on polygamy, simply Ann Louisa's predicament. "Come, Come Ye Saints" becomes her melody, in a theme and variations aria, found in the first act.[65]

At the end of the opera, as Brigham Young accepts Ann Louisa's decision to leave Deseret with her non-member beau, he sings this prophecy:

*This is God's plan, for someday Deseret too will go out into the great world .... As clearly as I once saw this valley long ago, As I stood upon the mountain and said "this is the place," I see Deseret, I see our people, our faith going out into the world.*[66]

The first performance of Handel's *Messiah* between Chicago and San Francisco was given in Salt Lake City in 1875 by George Careless with an ensemble of both Mormons and non-Mormons. It was an occasion of enormous musical impact. Critic Edward Tullidge wrote, "this .... *Messiah* is one of the capital events in the musical history of America."[67]

Squire Coop, born in Leeds, England, was another of Utah's musical visionaries. His work with the Ogden Tabernacle Choir was at times almost competitive with the Salt Lake Mormon Tabernacle Choir. In his later years he became Chair of Music at the University of California, Los Angeles. In 1901, armed with an LDS Missionary Permit, he studied piano with Leopold Godowsky in Berlin. He was in Bayreuth, Germany, and France, and in April of that same year he collected leaves from Giuseppe

Verdi's casket on the day of the Verdi funeral in Milan, Italy. Those leaves were mailed home to Utah.[68]

Annual performances of Handel's *Messiah* began in 1915, when The Oratorio Society of Utah was formed by Squire Coop. At that time, he was the first Chairman of the Department of Music at the University of Utah.[69] Those *Messiah* performances continue today. Soloists include local singers, but often outside guests.

One was baritone Richard Bonelli, who sang at the Metropolitan Opera from 1932–1945. Bonelli had a back story connecting him to Utah. In younger years, he had known a Spanish Fork Utahn by the name of Ab Jenkins. Jenkins served as mayor of Salt Lake City from 1940–1944. Both of them loved cars and became friends before Bonelli's star-turn in the opera world.[70]

Ab Jenkins set numerous world speed records, racing his *Mormon Meteor*. His accompaniment was Richard Bonelli, who would open up his operatic pipes and instigate a song fest, with the crowd joining him. Opera comes in many guises, but few could duplicate this one on Utah's Bonneville Salt Flats. It was Mayor Ab Jenkins, as an Oratorio Society board member, who brought Bonelli to sing *Messiah* solos in 1941 and 1942. Bonelli sang without a fee.[71]

Thomas Giles succeeded Squire Coop as Chair of Music at the University of Utah, serving from 1913–1948. His honed interests were opera and the piano, for which he trained in Berlin, Paris, Vienna, and Rome. From his arrival in 1913, operas were produced every year until World War II. Giuseppe Verdi's *Aïda* was given three times—first in 1916 in the Capitol Theatre. Subsequent performances were staged in 1926 and 1939, utilizing the outdoor pillared façade of the John R. Park Building as the setting.[72]

Not all operatic ventures in Utah were pleasant. In 1937, world-renowned African-American contralto Marian Anderson was refused a hotel room in Salt Lake City. In 1938, Hotel Utah provided a room, but only with her agreement to use the freight elevator. Finally, in 1948, accommodations were provided, no questions asked. Her Tabernacle concert was standing room only.[73]

In 1944 a young man from Idaho was serving in the U.S. Army. While stationed in North Africa, he was introduced to Madame Butterfly's aria, "*Un bel di*," by Giacomo Puccini. A transfer sent him to Italy, where the civilian administrator of the Allied Commission learned of this soldier's background in economics. He was soon named "Allied Controller of the

Italian Census Bureau," a position well-suited to his near doctoral education. The new assignment also came with perks more suited to high ranking officers. He was a Corporal. This led to the beginning of Leonard Arrington's:

> ... lifelong love affair with opera.... He rejoiced to learn that, given [t]his new position, the entire season was in his reach. "The errand boy stood in line for me all day to get me general admission tickets to the opera, ... and in the weeks that followed I went to 54 different operas in the Royal Opera House in Rome." (All on a salary of $67/month.)[74]

Leonard Arrington would later become one of the leading authorities on both Utah and Western American History and Church Historian for The Church of Jesus Christ of Latter-day Saints.

On January 16, 1931, a musician of 28 years conducted Verdi's *La forza del destino* in Kassel, Germany. He had never conducted *Forza* before, nor rehearsed it with the cast or orchestra. The general director of the Berlin State Opera was in attendance that night and made an offer which Maurice Abravanel accepted. There were specific instructions: "Take the night train to Berlin .... You rehearse with the singers in the morning. Tomorrow night you conduct *La Forza [del destino]* at the Berlin State Opera!" Abravanel would conduct there many times thereafter, each without rehearsal.[75] Verdi's *Force of Destiny* continued to play its hand.

World War II took Abravanel from Germany to France, Australia, and New York City where, in 1936, at the age of 33, he became the youngest conductor ever signed by the Metropolitan Opera. There, he set the record of conducting seven performances of five different operas in nine days.[76] In 1947, Maurice Abravanel came to Salt Lake City with a one-year contract to conduct the Utah State Symphony Orchestra.

Broadway notable Arnold Sundgaard had written the book for a new musical, *Promised Valley*. The music was being written by the young Crawford Gates. *Promised Valley* celebrated the pioneer centennial and was given in the stadium at the University of Utah with a success beyond expectations. Its star was Alfred Drake, the original Curly in Rodgers and Hammerstein's *Oklahoma*.[77]

With the University Stadium now fully production-ready, Maurice Abravanel and others produced the first Summer Festival in 1948. The idea succeeded and continued through 1965. Festival repertoire included operas like *The Tales of Hoffman, Carmen, Der Rosenkavalier,* and *Salome*. Significant artists came to sing the big roles, including a still unknown

Beverly Sills, who sang *Naughty Marietta* and *La traviata* in 1953 and returned for *Aïda* in 1954.[78]

As the Summer Festival progressed, Abravanel invited the young Ardean Watts to coach *Salome,* beginning the next morning. Having seen the Strauss opera all of once in Vienna, Watts accepted. Then he spent the night in preparation, writing jazz short-hand notes into the orchestral score. His success was such that after 1965, Ardean Watts led a broad repertoire of professional performances by the University of Utah Opera Company in Kingsbury Hall.[79]

In 1968, Watts commissioned James Prigmore to write "The Rise of the Gods, or the Downfall of Wagner."[80] Fond memories remain for those who experienced the use of Wagner-like motives, borrowed from popular television shows and commercials of the time and cleverly adapted into this Wagnerian spoof performed with members of the Utah Symphony.[81]

Besides Ardean Watts, Abravanel influenced a number of Utah musicians. Ariel Bybee was a soprano from BYU. Maurice Abravanel conducted her as Violetta (Verdi's *La traviata*) in Salt Lake City and had her perform and record with the Utah Symphony. He took her to the Music Academy of the West in Santa Barbara, California, where she worked with the legendary Lotte Lehmann.[82] Next, she was off to San Francisco Opera where no less than Martin Bernheimer wrote of her, "Hats off, gentlemen, a Carmen!—Her name is Ariel Bybee ... ."[83]

In 1977, Ms. Bybee went to the Metropolitan Opera, where she eventually sang 460 performances. Perhaps her finest portrayal was Jenny in *The Rise and Fall of the City of Mahagonny,* by Kurt Weill. Critic Barton Wimble wrote:

> Bybee was sensational, not only vocally but in her look and her grasp of the role.... Her vocal command ... was superb.... The role of Jenny tops with a C and she handled everything with a bright, focused tone and a tight but not unpleasant vibrato that added urgency to the part.... From now on, the role of Jenny will have to be judged against her definitive interpretation.[84]

In 1928 the LDS Church had entered into an agreement to produce a silent film titled *All Faces West.* The arrival of talking pictures blindsided the project. Roland Parry from Weber College was hired to compose music in an effort that failed to salvage the film.[85]

Later, the city of Ogden wanted a musical project, and *All Faces West* became a new pioneer musical. It premiered in 1951 and ran for 17 summers, including a tour to New Zealand. Roland Parry wrote the music and the text was by his wife, Helen Talmage Parry.

Remembering Alfred Drake in *Promised Valley*, Ogden went after Mario Lanza to play Brigham Young. Lanza wasn't available, and the role went to the Ukrainian-American baritone, Igor Gorin.[86] The city of Ogden had a hit. In 1956, BYU recognized Igor Gorin with an honorary degree—Doctor of Public Service in Music.[87]

Gorin sang *All Faces West* excerpts on his tours. An entire *Bell Telephone Hour* was devoted to it. Its producer, Wallace McGill, said, "I have the album and I can't count the times I've played the Prayer. This music .... has a certain spiritual quality which I find difficult to describe."[88]

In June 1947, some 13 years before the *Force of Destiny* would catch up with Leonard Warren at the Metropolitan Opera, he appeared with the Tabernacle Choir in celebration of the centennial arrival of the Mormon Pioneers. Lowell Durham wrote, "Warren took his audience by surprise and storm—the greatest baritone voice ever to be heard locally."[89]

JoAnn Ottley was Utah's treasured soprano in the latter 20th century. In Utah, her operas included *Bohème, Rigoletto, Fledermaus, Traviata,* and *Lucia.* Her eleventh -hour substitution with the Utah Symphony for the ailing Roberta Peters is fabled. She had a voice of exquisite beauty, delivered with equal musicality. From her student days, she recalled a late night phone call from the Utah Symphony about their indisposed soprano. Could she *immediately* come to the Tabernacle to sing the high C in the recording session for the Mahler 8th Symphony? She rescued that recording session and received a check for $25 as payment for those high C.[90]

Tenor Glade Peterson had been a part of Abravanel's Summer Festival operas before spending 12 years as principal tenor in Zurich, Switzerland. He sang in most of the major houses of the world, including Paris, Milan, Hamburg, Vienna, the Salzburg Festival, Houston Grand Opera, San Francisco Opera, and the Metropolitan.

In the mid-1970's, Glade Peterson returned home and set about establishing Utah Opera. The late Ardean Watts considered it "a friendly takeover of his University of Utah Opera Company."[91] The challenges were enormous. Always a horseman, Glade did his fundraising on horseback.[92] Daynes Music donated the initial office space. Then the Capitol Theatre became home for the new company, which opened in 1978 with Puccini's *La bohème.*[93] The 2017–18 season celebrates Utah Opera's 40th anniversary.

Buffalo Bill's Cherry wood bar—Irma Hotel Grill, Cody, Wyoming (photo credit: Walter B. Rudolph)

Logan's Utah Festival Opera and Music Theatre exists because of the vision of Michael Ballam, another successful Utah operatic tenor. *Summerhays* is one of the noted musical families in Utah, and Ballam therein resides.[94] Restoring first what is now the Ellen Eccles Theatre, he followed it with the Dansante Building and then remodeled the Utah Theatre. The five-week season in July and August provides one of America's unique festival settings. Celebrating 25 years in 2017, the very first tickets sold when it opened in 1993 were purchased by Leonard Arrington. Later, Michael Ballam and JoAnn Ottley would both sing at Leonard Arrington's funeral.[95]

Among those Utahns who have written operas, two more must be mentioned. In *Orpheus Lex,* by Marie Nelson Bennett, Orpheus and Euridice are living in a cabin in Idaho. The key for Orpheus is to not remember Euridice by not looking back in time. The use of popular songs, plus the Idaho setting for the Greek myth, provides an operatic experience of novel originality. The libretto is by another Utahn, David Kranes.[96]

Murray Boren, retired composer-in-residence at BYU, has several operas to his credit. These include *Emma,* the story of Emma Smith following the martyrdom of her husband. The libretto was written by Eric Samuelsen.[97] *The Book of Gold* details the challenges Joseph Smith felt during the translation of *the Book of Mormon,* with a libretto by Glen Nelson. Boren uses a gripping musical language that is thoroughly matched to the historical

The Cherry wood bar, constructed for the Robert Carsen production of *La fanciulla del West* (Giacomo Puccini) (Teatro alla Scala, Milan, Italy, May 2016). (photo credit: Marco Brescia, Teatro alla Scala)

action of the librettos. That the topics are LDS in no way diminishes the strength of his operatic expression.

Naming significant Utah singers active today is a bit like Lenski challenging Eugene Onegin to a duel. One would be astonished at any list, and it would always have glaring omissions. I don't relish a duel, and I provide

The Miners greet and cheer *La fanciulla del West*, by Giacomo Puccini in Monument Valley, Utah (Teatro alla Scala, Milan, Italy, May 2016). (photo credit: Marco Brescia, Teatro alla Scala)

no list. Suffice it to say, there are outstanding singers with Utah connections appearing in major opera houses all over the world. They honor Utah, and we are proud of their achievements.

During a period of online research, I encountered a link to a review of the recent production of Giacomo Puccini's *La fanciulla del West,* premiered by La Scala Opera in May 2016. I knew there was nothing in that review pertaining to my research, yet I was compelled to open it. In a quick scan I found references to Buffalo Bill's Irma Hotel at Cody, and a sunburned view of Monument Valley (Utah).[98]

The Puccini score says it takes place in 19th century Gold Rush, California, so I questioned the editor of TheOperaCritic.com, Michael Sinclair. He wrote to the noted director and co-designer, Robert Carsen, for clarity. Carsen replied to me:

> I based [my] design ... for the Act 1 bar, on Cody's [cherry wood] bar in the Irma Hotel, which I visited ... when I was preparing to write and direct Buffalo Bill's Wild West Show for the opening of Euro Disney in Paris.

The cherry wood bar was a gift from Queen Victoria to Buffalo Bill Cody. Now it became scenery for Puccini's opera at La Scala in Milan:

[The opera] production was a[n] homage to the genre of Western cinema.... [It] starts with some men ... watching a Western. [As] the film ends ... the cinema is turned into a version of the famous [cherry wood] bar at the Irma.... [When] the Girl herself appears, we are in the middle of a wrap-around [film] view of Monument Valley [Utah].[99]

At the opera's end, the miners bid the Girl of the Golden West "goodbye" as she leaves with her 'movie-star boyfriend,' riding off into the Utah Sunset.

Robert Carsen's cinematic idea with this production of *La fanciulla del West* identifies one final 'operatic voice in Utah'—the state itself.

\* \* \*

Now, the final questions.

First, who will continue this research? Much has been omitted here, and there is much more to be discovered and written!

And second, was it Puccini's *Fanciulla del West,* or Mozart's *Don Giovanni?* I'm referring to the one who goes to Hell for bad behavior. In one production Giovanni was lowered to his reward on a small elevator, which stuck... On a second attempt, Giovanni was halfway into Hell when it stuck again, prompting a shout from the balcony, "Great Scott! Hell is full!"

It seems we are left with two choices. I say, "let Hell be full—I'm sticking with *The Girl of the Golden West.* Won't you join me, riding off into the Utah Sunset to our 'happily ever after,' naturally, at the opera!"

# ENDNOTES

1.  *La forza del destino* by Giuseppe Verdi (cancelled performance, March 4, 1960), Metropolitan Opera Archives, http://archives.metoperafamily.org/archives/scripts/cgiip.exe/WService =BibSpeed/fullcit.w?xCID=184330.
2.  *La forza del destino* by Giuseppe Verdi (broadcast performance, March 22, 1975), Metropolitan Opera Archives, http://69.18.170.204/archives/scripts/cgiip.exe/WService=BibSpeed/fullcit.w ?xCID=240900&limit=3000&xBranch=ALL&xsdate=&xedate=&theterm=1974-75&x=0&x homepath=http://69.18.170.204/archives/&xhome=http://69.18.170.204/archives/bibpro .htm.
3.  Kaufmann, Jonas, "La dolce vita," *Jonas Kaufmann: My Italy*, DVD, Sony Classical MSWK537164BR, April 7, 2017.
4.  Tullidge, Edward W., *History of Salt Lake City*, (Salt Lake City: Star Publishing, 1885), 768.
5.  Lindsay, John S., *The Mormons and the Theatre or the History of Theatricals in Utah* (Salt Lake City: Century Printing, 1905), 5–6.
6.  Tullidge, *History of Salt Lake City*, 770–1.
7.  Van Leer, Twila, "Salt Lake Theatre was Star of the Western Stage," *The Deseret News*, January 28, 1996.
8.  Tullidge, *History of Salt Lake City*, 772–3.
9.  Lindsay, *The Mormons and the Theatre*, 41.
10. Maxwell, David, "The Morning Breaks: George Careless, Musical Pioneer," *Ensign*, February 1984.
11. Pyper, George D., "In Intimate Touch with Professor George Careless, II," *The Juvenile Instructor*, April 1924, 174.
12. Pyper, George D., "In Intimate Touch with Professor George Careless, II," 174–76.
13. Tullidge, *History of Salt Lake City*, 778.
14. Mitchell, Robert C., "The Desert Tortoise," *Utah Historical Quarterly* 35, no. 4 (Fall 1967): 281.
15. Cone, John Frederick, *Adelina Patti: Queen of Hearts* (Portland, OR: Amadeus Press, 1993), 129.
16. Rosenthal, Harold, ed., *The Mapleson Memoirs* (New York: Appleton-Century, 1966), 193–4, 208.
17. "Patti, the World's Great Diva Electrifies a Salt Lake Audience," *Salt Lake Herald*, April 2, 1884.
18. Hanson, Basil, *An Historic Account of Music Criticism and Music Critics in Utah* (thesis), L. Tom Perry Special Collections, Harold B. Lee Library, Brigham Young University, Provo, Utah, May 1933, 107. See also James, Edward T., ed. *Notable American Women–A Biographical Dictionary* (Cambridge, MA: Belknap Press, 1971), 149.

19. Whitney, Horace C., *Drama in Utah* (Salt Lake City: *The Deseret News*, 1915), 37, 41–43.
20. Menand, Louis, "Crooner in Rights Spat: Are Copyright Laws Too Strict?" *The New Yorker*, October 20, 2015.
21. Parshall, Ardis, E., "Deseret: The Opera–Act 1," *The Keepapitchinin*, October 17, 2011, http://www.keepapitchinin.org/2011/10/17/deseret-the-opera-act-i/.
22. Nelson, Glen, "Mormons, Opera and Mormon Operas," *The Deseret News*, January 17, 2009.
23. Parshall, "Deseret: The Opera," *The Keepapitchinin*.
24. Whitney, *Drama in Utah*, 41.
25. Pyper, George D., *The Romance of an Old Playhouse* (Salt Lake City: Seagull Press, 1928), 319, 327.
26. Parshall, Ardis, E., "The Loveliest Missionary Tract Ever Published," *The Keepapitchinin*, December 28, 2008, http://www.keepapitchinin.org/2008/12/28/the-loveliest-missionary -tract-ever-published/.
27. *The Latter-Day Saints' Millennial Star*, 63, August 1, 1901, 508–9.
28. Pyper, *The Romance of an Old Playhouse*, 327.
29. Hicks, Michael, *The Mormon Tabernacle Choir: A Biography* (Urbana, Chicago, and Springfield: University of Illinois Press, 2015), 49.
30. *The New York Times*, February 5, 1902.
31. Harrison, Conrad B., "She's Utah's First Lady of Music," *The Deseret News*, October 10, 1948.
32. Coray, John Louis, *Emma Lucy Gates (Bowen): Her Accomplishments in Opera and Concert* (thesis), L. Tom Perry Special Collections, Harold B. Lee Library, Brigham Young University, Provo, Utah, July 1956, 78–79.
33. Coray, *Emma Lucy Gates (Bowen)*, 65, 100–1.
34. Offenbach, Jacques, "The Doll Song," *The Tales of Hoffman*, Columbia 78 rpm record (Columbia A3326), recording courtesy of the L. Tom Perry Special Collections, Harold B. Lee Library, Brigham Young University, Provo, Utah.
35. "Finest Voice upon Stage, Tribute Paid Lucy Gates," *Salt Lake Telegram*, September 27, 1919.
36. Tullidge, *History of Salt Lake City*, 782–83.
37. "*Parsifal* Tonight," *Ogden Standard Examiner*, November 5, 1908.
38. "*Parsifal* Tonight," *Ogden Standard Examiner*, February 22, 1906.
39. *Logan Republican*, October 20, 1906.
40. *Logan Republican*, October 20, 1906; October 14, 1908.
41. *The Deseret Evening News*, November 7, 1908.
42. "With the First Nighters," *Goodwin's Weekly*, November 14, 1908.
43. "Last Organ Recital," *Salt Lake Tribune*, October 2, 1907.
44. Hicks, *The Mormon Tabernacle Choir: A Biography*, 159.
45. Hicks, *The Mormon Tabernacle Choir: A Biography*, 179.
46. Lindsay, *The Mormons and the Theatre*, 79–80.
47. Pyper, *The Romance of an Old Playhouse*, 324.
48. Jackson, Paul, *Saturday Afternoons at the Old Met, 1931–50* (Portland, OR: Amadeus Press, 1992), 5.
49. "Members of the Marconi Opera Company Who Will Sing *La Bohème* for Monday's K.D.Y.L. Concert," *Salt Lake Telegram*, September 23, 1922.
50. Pyper, *The Romance of an Old Playhouse*, 329.
51. Mitchell, "The Desert Tortoise," 283.
52. "Chaliapin Coming Here January 27," *Salt Lake Telegram*, January 2, 1927.
53. Mitchell, Robert C., "The Desert Tortoise," 283.
54. "Orders Pour in to Hear Noted Tenor," *Ogden Standard Examiner*, November 4, 1945.
55. Ekman, Lennart, email to the author, November 2012. (Johanna Hanna Eleonora Sund, born July 7, 1833 in Stora Tuna, Sweden, died November 19, 1922 in Draper, Utah, USA.)
56. Dalton, David, interview with the author, April 2017.
57. Richards, LeGrand Jr., interview with the author, April 2017.
58. Dalton, David and Donna, eds. "Concerts & Lectures, under Brigham Young University Lyceum Series, 1921–1971." A list of visiting artists to BYU, presented by Herald R. Clark.

Copy provided by the editors. See also Davidson, Karen Lynn, interview with the author, April 12, 2017.

59. Hipster, Edward Ellsworth, *American Opera and Its Composers* (Philadelphia: Theodore Presser Co., 1934), 245–49.

60. Peterson, Nancy M., "From the Heart of Chaos: Finding Zitkala-Ša," in *The Way West: True Stories of the American Frontier*, edited by James A. Crutchfield (New York: Tom Doherty Associates LLC, 2005), 223.

61. Hanson, William F., "I Have Two Little Hands," *Children's Songbook* (Salt Lake City: Corporation of the President of The Church of Jesus Christ of Latter-day Saints, 1989), 272.

62. Quinn, D. Michael, *Elder Statesman: A Biography of J. Reuben Clark* (Salt Lake City: Signature Books, 2002), 368, 370.

63. Clark, J. Reuben, Jr., "Funeral Services Program," October 10, 1961, L. Tom Perry Special Collections, Harold B. Lee Library, Brigham Young University.

64. Nelson, Valerie J., "Anne H. Bailey, 82; Writer in Opera, Soaps," *Los Angeles Times,* November 30, 2006.

65. Kastle, Leonard, "Ann Louisa's Aria," *Deseret*, opera in 3 acts, libretto by Anne Howard Bailey, piano/vocal score, private printing owned by BYU Opera Workshop, 33–46. See also Kastle, Leonard, NBC Opera Theatre's *Deseret* (sound recording), https://www.youtube.com/watch?v=V3o-jEcpqnI.

66. Kastle, Leonard, *Deseret*, piano/vocal score, *Brigham Young's Closing Solo*, 292–98. See also *Deseret* (sound recording), https://www.youtube.com/watch?v=V3o-jEcpqnI.

67. Tullidge, *History of Salt Lake City*, 775.

68. Smith, Marcus Sidney, *With Them Were Ten Thousand and More: The Authorized History of The Oratorio Society of Utah* (Salt Lake City: Actaeon Books, 1989), 65.

69. Smith, *With Them Were Ten Thousand and More,* 98.

70. Noeth, Louise Ann, "Ab Jenkins–Our Father, Who Art of the Salt ... ," *SAE International,* http://motorsports.sae.org/articles/guest/abjenkins.htm.

71. "Oratorio Society Offers Tickets Free for *The Messiah*," *Salt Lake Telegram*, December 23, 1941.

72. *The Deseret News,* February 2, 1959, p. B-9. See also *The Deseret News,* Sunday May 23, 1948, p. F.3; Smith, *With Them Were Ten Thousand and More*, 52–53.

73. Alexander, Thomas, "The Civil Rights Movement," *Utah, the Right Place*, https://heritage.utah.gov/history/uhg-civil-rights-movement-utah.

74. Prince, Gregory A., *Leonard Arrington and the Writing of Mormon History* (Salt Lake City: University of Utah Press, 2016), 44–46.

75. Durham, Lowell, *Abravanel* (Salt Lake City: University of Utah Press, 1989), 11.

76. Durham, *Abravanel*, 21–2.

77. "*Promised Valley*—a Musical Epic Every Utahn Should See," *Salt Lake Telegram*, July 23, 1947.

78. Sills, Beverly, "From First Note to Last," http://www.beverlysillsonline.com/annals/Sillslist.php?search=salt+lake+city.

79. Watts, Ardean, interview with the author, January 10, 2017.

80. Prigmore, James, interview with the author, April 4, 2017.

81. "Opera to Appeal to Doubters," *The Chronicle*, May 16, 1968.

82. Bybee, Ariel, interview with the author, May 5, 2017.

83. Bernheimer, Martin, "Review of *Carmen*," *The Los Angeles Times*, February 28, 1973.

84. Wimble, Barton, "Review of *The Rise and Fall of the City of Mahagony*, Metropolitan Opera," *New York Daily News*, March 31–April 1, 1981.

85. Lewis, George Edward, *All Faces West*, 35 mm film, *Mormon Literature & Creative Arts*, http://mormonarts.lib.byu.edu/works/all-faces-west.

86. Rudolph, Walter B., *All Faces West*, KBYU-FM radio documentary interview with Gloria Parry Walter, July 15, 1997.

87. BYU Commencement program, June 1, 1956, https://archive.org/stream/commencementexer1956brig#page/16/mode/1up.

88. McGill, Wallace, sound recording in possession of David Fillman, trustee for Igor and Mary Gorin Trust. See also Sound recording, "All Faces West" 10 inch LP, Pargo Records VLP 31.

89.  Durham, Lowell papers, courtesy of Roger Miller.

90.  Ottley, JoAnn, interview with the author, May 5, 2017.

91.  Watts, Ardean, interview with the author, January 10, 2017.

92.  Peterson, Leslie, interview with the author, January 30, 2017.

93.  Harris, Sarah, "Utah Opera Celebrates 40th Anniversary," *The Deseret News*, September 18, 2017. See also Miller, Roger, interview with the author, February 23, 2017; private papers from Roger Miller.

94.  Stowe, Dorothy, "Summerhays: A Pioneer Legacy," *Deseret News*, July 23, 1995.

95.  Ballam, Michael, interview with the author, April 28, 2017. Ottley, JoAnn, interview with the author, May 5, 2017.

96.  Bennett, Marie Nelson, "CD notes to *Orpheus Lex*," Ravello Records (CD) RR 7885.

97.  Kozinn, Allan, "Mormons in Crisis after Their Founder's Death," *The New York Times*, July 14, 1992, http://www.nytimes.com/1992/07/14/news/review-opera-mormons-in-crisis-after -their-founder-s-death.html.

98.  Luraghi, Silvia, "*La fanciulla del West* as Spaghetti Western," *Teatro all Scala*, May 7, 2016, *theoperacritic.com*, https://theoperacritic.com/tocreviews2.php?review=sl/2016/milfanciu 0516.html.

99.  Carsen, Robert, email exchange with the author, May 21–June 16, 2017.

# ADDENDUM

The following text was written to both tease and honor Dr. Arrington. It seems appropriately included here.

"The Modern Church Historian" is to be sung to the tune "I am the very Model of a Modern Major General," from *The Pirates of Penzance* by Gilbert and Sullivan.

It is reprinted by permission from the authors, Jill Mulvay Derr and Paul L. Anderson. It also is found in Gregory A. Prince, *Leonard Arrington and the Writing of Mormon History*, pp. 91–3.

I am the very model of a modern Church Historian,
In matters economical, doctrinal, and folklorian.
I know the Mormon leaders and I write their prosopography
With research that enlarges and illumines their biography.

I've studied men and women both quixotic and mercurial,
I tend to favor those like me, somewhat entrepreneurial.
I've drawn my own conclusions about Brigham Young's maturity
And analyzed investments of the Eccles' First Security.

(Chorus)
He's analyzed investments of the Eccles' First Security,
He's analyzed investments of the Eccles' First Security,
He's analyzed investments of the Eccles' First Securi-curity.

I've also dabbled quite a little bit in social history,
The arts and letters of the Saints provide a lot of grist for me.

Since I can chant "Come, Come Ye Saints" just like a true gregorian
I am the very model of a modern Church Historian.

> (Chorus)
> Since he can chant "Come, Come Ye Saints" just like a true gregorian
> He is the very model of a modern Church Historian.

I'm very good at research and I know historiography
As well as hermeneutics and statistical demography.
I know the folklore: the Three Nephites, and Jim Bridger's ears of corn,
The so-called White Horse Prophecy and Porter Rockwell's locks unshorn.

I'm awfully well acquainted too with matters economical
In this Great Basin Kingdom throughout all its chronological
Development, I understand its finances and enterprise.
I've counted ev'ry thing in sight from Sunday eggs to railroad ties.

> (Chorus)
> He's counted ev'ry thing in sight from Sunday eggs to railroad ties. (etc.)

I'm very well acquainted too with issues in theology,
I understand statistics, mystics and phenomenology.
Since I can Bible bash with any Institute scriptorian
I am the very model of a modern Church Historian.

> (Chorus)
> Since he can Bible bash with any Institute scriptorian
> He is the very model of a modern Church Historian.

In fact, when I can write a book devoid of all tendentiousness,
Accept awards and accolades without the least pretentiousness,
When I have learned the ins and outs of writing up a grant request,
When I explain with utmost tact polygamy post-manifest,

When I can smell a controversy brewing and put up my guards,
When I can spot a phony Salamander at a hundred yards,
When I am granted access to the archives of the DUP,
Then I'll deserve a pardon and an honorary PhD.

> (Chorus)
> Then he'll deserve a pardon and an honorary PhD. (etc.)

When I learn that I need more than a scholar's normal bag of tricks,
Especially a healthy grasp of bureaucratic politics,
In matters economical, political, folklorian,
I'll be the very model of a modern Church Historian.

(Chorus)
In matters economical, political, folklorian,
He'll be the very model of a modern Church Historian.